The Night Won't Save Anyone

The Night
Won't Save Anyone

POEMS BY
MARCIA SOUTHWICK

Athens
The University of Georgia Press

Copyright © 1980 by the University of Georgia Press
Athens, Georgia 30602

All rights reserved

Set in 10 on 12 point Monticello type
Printed in the United States of America

Library of Congress Cataloging in Publication Data

Southwick, Marcia.
    The night won't save anyone.
    I. Title.
PS3569.O83N5   813'.54   80–11968
ISBN 0–8203–0519–7
ISBN 0–8203–0520–0 pbk.

for Larry and Nicholas

The publication of this book is supported by a grant from the National Endowment for the Arts, a federal agency.

Acknowledgments

The author and the publisher gratefully acknowledge the following publications in which poems from this volume first appeared.

American Poetry Review: "I Awaken" (under the title "What the Trees Go Into")
Antaeus: "No Such Thing"
Carolina Quarterly: "Vasilisa the Beautiful"
Crazy Horse: "The Land As It Is"
The Georgia Review: "A Burial, Green"
Intro 10: The second stanza of "Poem in Which I Am an Old Woman" appeared as part of "In the Open"
New Letters: "My Husband and I Share a Nightmare"
The North American Review: "A Song of Drowning"
The Ohio Review: "Kaspar Hauser"
Open Places: "Thaisa," "Once My Husband Gave Me a Horse" (under the title "The Woman Who Buried a Stone")
Ploughshares: "Dusk"; the first stanza of "Poem in Which I Am an Old Woman" appeared as part of "Finches"
Poetry: "Landscape," "Owning a Dead Man," "Winter Gulls," "The Night Won't Save Anyone"
Seneca Review: "Passionately"

"The Marsh" and "Beneath the Beech Trees" (under the title "Reminiscence") first appeared in *Five Missouri Poets*, copyright © 1979 by Chariton Review Press and Northeast Missouri State University.
"Owning a Dead Man" was reprinted in *The Anthology of Magazine Verse and Yearbook of American Poetry*, 1980.
"Thaisa" and other poems appeared as a limited edition pamphlet printed by Singing Wind Publications, 1980.
"What the Trees Go Into" appeared as a limited edition pamphlet printed by Burning Deck Press, 1977.
"Upon Hearing of a Drowning in the Connecticut River" first appeared as the title poem of a chapbook in the Inland Boat series published by Porch Publications, 1980.

Special thanks to Philip Levine and James Randall for their help and encouragement.

Contents

IV · The Night Won't Save Anyone

I

What the Trees Go Into

it was never written, not even in symbols, for this they knew—
no secret was safe with a woman.

H.D.

The last snow
is lifting itself off the awnings
and I am thinking

if anything is bleeding
I do not see it.

In some ways
I am like the woman
who sends out her soul
in the form of a wasp

and in some ways
you are like the man
who catches the wasp.

When he closes his hand,
she sleeps.
When he opens his hand,
she wakes.

Now I can hear the rain
being quietly released
like grains from a sack,

and I can hear you talking:
the tribes
who molded their skulls for beauty
used instruments
no more ingenious
than the common mousetrap

and remember,
in some villages
when the hunters leave
they make their women sleep
facing the direction
of their departure

and Goodnight; then you leave,
tying a live bird
to my bedpost.

Promise me something.
Tomorrow, when you come back
to release the bird,
please make it carry
my fever along with it.

The boys constructed
a wooden image of a bird.
It revolved on a pivot,
and it sang for us.

A musician played
a long horn,
though after the music was over,
we knew the horn would be broken
or buried.

My mother said:
name the first born
after the first person
who enters your house;

take the second one
up in your arms
as it cries, and rock it,
saying different names;

the name at which the child
stops crying
is the right one.

My father promised me
a new dress,
but that was not enough.

5

He promised me
a sway-backed horse, and said:
you have to be content with this.

I stood in the yard
waiting to leave;
the horse was stamping in the place
where the groom had passed . . .

My parents waved and called
Goodbye.

And as we left,
we could see the trees ahead
growing smaller,
the spaces between them
too narrow to go through.

The barren women still roll
under the trees and do not sing . . .

I have sons who hang their clothes
in the trees

hoping the dead will slip
into the garments they recognize

and I say: you can break a few
of your belongings
to scatter over the graves, that's all.

You can give them these
and nothing more.

*

I spoke quietly,
I was not alone—

once, my husband gave me a horse;
he led it gently
through the faded grass.

I could hear one hoof
hit the gravel, then the second
and he said: Eskimos offer

fresh water to the seals,
oil to the birds,
arrows to the bears,

I will give you this horse
if you promise to ride away on it.

*

At the river, the children bathe
and turn away in the water.

The river is humming all around them;
their voices slide across the water.

On the bank, a lizard crawls out
from beneath a rock. It stares
and its body swells like a tiny black purse.

Even as it blinks, it stares
at the inside of its own eyelids.

*

I return to the town. The people
are building a house, and while I sleep

they measure my body. They place
the measurement under the stone.

They believe this will make
the building last forever.

Tomorrow, I will bury another stone
under the first. You can look all you like,

but this stone can burrow
faster than a man can dig . . .

    *

When the dead pass, the women do not sweep.
They cut locks of hair to lay in the road.
The children go to look for fire; they sing.

The dead come down to eat fish, ascending again
in the smoke of the fires they make—

and what they sing, no one can remember.

9

I must have been dreaming.
Someone was following me across a lake
covered with ice, and the ice broke.

I was dreaming, too,
of children who were stillborn,
though they had memories.

    In heaven, the candles went out
    one by one.

What does this mean?
One of the children told me
his history, the history
a womb can have,
and his mother's history,
and his grandmother's,
until he reached the last ancestor
he could remember,
and that was me.

In the dream I grew angry.
I strangled the child
and put him in a sack.
I took the sack to a lake
to throw it in,
but the lake was covered with ice.

In the distance I could see
someone running, his feet

slipping sideways across the ice,
and another man was following,
wearing a helmet of fire,
wearing a cloak of birds,
I couldn't tell.

   In heaven, there were only crows
   sitting on branches,
   and the branches were carried by men
   until it looked like a whole forest
   filled with crows
   was moving toward me.

   The men said nothing.
   They set down the branches quietly
   and the crows flew off.
   The sky was filled with beaks,
   and the men were grinning.

On the other side of the lake
the trees were moving,
though there was no wind.
I dug a hole in the ice.
As I looked down,
I could see myself in the water.
I was much older than I am.

When I looked up,
the trees were gone—
only a row of men

standing at the lake's edge.
So I took up the sack
with the stillborn in it
and went home, back to bed,
where I used the sack for a pillow.

Then the men took candles
out of their pockets and lit them
as they moved toward me,
and I blew them all out
like a kind of birthday
for the dead,

and I began to run
over the lake,
the ice cracking around me.
The men didn't follow
but I knew they were grinning.

I grew tired, running,
and so cold I couldn't
move anymore.
So I fell asleep
on the lake;
the crows covered me
with their extra feathers
until I was a little warmer.

Then I woke up here,
next to you.

But that's impossible.
Next to me is the wind

    which sees without candles.
    To the wind these words
    are dice.

My son wakes me
and says mother
the birds never arrive,
they die in mid-air.

Listen closely,
do you hear their bones
falling to the ground?

No and I get up,
smoothing away the impression
my body makes on the bed.

*

My daughter
throws her dolls
into the river;

she says mother
I can feel a shadow coming,
longer than this river

(a crocodile
drags her reflection
under the water)

and it is not a shadow,
it is what the trees
go into.

*

A nightmare sat
like a bird
on my chest:

now I am a bird
but I used to be like you—
a young married woman
who liked to knit.

Really, you are a weasel
and you are envious
as you enter the closet
to destroy my dresses.

*

I take the children to town
where a puppet
representing the oldest woman

is carried through the square
and sawn in half;

if I die, don't be afraid.
Before I rise,
I will waste plenty of time

counting the grains of barley
you scatter over my grave.

*

I know there's a heavy rain
no one can fix.

Before it arrives,
it passes
through the numb hearts
of the dead;

it soaks their clothes
until they wake.
It almost drowns them.

*

I know I will take up my needle
and stretch a thread over the water

so the dead can cross safely
hand over hand.

I know my body
from water.

I know my hands
from shells.

I know my eyes
from fish eyes

and my skin
from moss.

I know this water
isn't a window
I can open.

*

The wind is no help.
It parts the hair,
it divides the grass,
it ruffles the fur
on the back of a weasel,

it divides everything I say
into three parts water
and one part earth.

Water turns wood to stone;
it turns the drowned to stone.

17

Water can fossilize a drowned woman's dress,
and the dress is heavy with embroidery,
and now the embroidery is hard as cartilage.

*

The dead can dig without arms.
They go deeper
until they gather
by an underground stream
and tell stories.

There is no sky left
in their skulls,
though there is rain

and whole palaces
in ruins,
in which women are carrying
bouquets of flowers,

and people celebrate
by piling the flowers
in a deserted ballroom
on a marble floor so shiny
the petals
are multiplied,

and they burn the flowers
and dance

in and out of the smoke,
singing . . .

These are the songs
I remember as I drown—

I am singing to scare you off.
This water is mine.

II
Fables

Death is our Evil. The Gods believe this,
or else by now they would be dead.

Sappho

Kaspar Hauser

A boy abandoned by his parents and raised in a cell
by a prison guard

All day I play alone with two wooden horses
and a few ribbons. I rearrange the horses,
hanging the ribbons from them
in different positions.

In my little cell, I try to imagine my parents,
and I can see a lamp hanging from a wagon,
and my parents, in the distance,
driving some horses in winter.

They are passing a deer buried in the snow,
though only the deer's antlers are visible,
and by the river, they are passing an otter
with its eyes closed, eating a salmon.

Now I can see the wagon more clearly, as it moves
out of the woods, and slowly up the street of the town,
where I am standing on my corner, waiting . . .

The bells on the harness make so little noise,
only the dead should know who is coming . . .

And I stand here, holding up my toys,
because when my parents pass,
I always think they will know,
by my wooden horses, who I am.

Doppelgänger

You're waiting somewhere,
outside of town, memorizing
my gestures, reading the books
I've read, eating the food
I've eaten, wearing the clothes
I used to wear,
fitting your too flat feet
into my shoes,
your too large hands
wet as seaweed, into my gloves,
pulling my favorite hat
over the tangled hair,
over one eye,
the eye that mocks mine,
a green in reverse
like a dead sea. You stick
to me like a burr,
cling to me
like a blight on a crop. You
are my lazy sister
mowing down wheat
while drinking whiskey
out of little jars. I'd like
to give you something,
a token of my esteem,
but I can't shop in these fields
forever. And this
is where you'll die,
out here, under the stars,
and no one will hear you

when your heart goes
into another gear.
And the heart whirs
like five engines
and goes out.

Vasilisa the Beautiful
from the Russian fairytale

1

What's the use?
There's nothing wonderful
about being so beautiful.
For my sisters,
I do all the work.

Start a fire,
mix the dough,
wash the plates,
milk the cow!
They knit

by the light of a single splinter
of birch,
and when the light goes out
they knit in the dark,
the needles still glowing.

2

Find us light!
I walk through the wood
to a witch's hut,
a hut that spins
on fowls' legs.

Now I work for the witch.
I prepare the meals:
a pot of *borsht*

and half a cow,
twenty chickens

and a roasted sow,
cider and mead
and home-brewed ale,
beer by the barrel
and *kvass* by the pail.

3

I have a little doll.
It tells me what to do:
take a skull from the witch's fence
and hide it
beneath the worm-eaten roses.

But I go home.
I carry the skull on a stick.
The eyes can glow,
so I see my way.
My sisters won't know.

They're alone in the house.
The skull's on fire!
The fire's a wish
my sisters don't have.
And the wish burns.

Passionately

after a poem by Paul Eluard

1

In the grass
The sky
The road
In the linen hanging between houses
She played everywhere
Like someone drowning

I wanted to change everything

As she stood motionless
I would close around her
The impossible
Heavy doors

2

The laugh after it played made a butterfly escape
From a table already sailing

3

She tore off her dress
Beginning to be nude
She embraced a mirror

4

In the vault of autumn
From coal and thunder

She gradually made
A flower resembling snow

5

The house in the city
The earth in the house
And on the earth a woman
And in her eye
A child a mirror water and fire

6

She could live alone
Because of her youth
I did not know how to confine
My heart to its single chest

7

There is nothing but this delicate face
There is nothing but this delicate bird
Far off on the pier where children become weak

At the parting of winter
When clouds begin to burn
When new air takes on its color
As always

There is nothing but this infancy flying in front of life.

Thaisa

1

They place me gently
in a blue and gold sea-room
no one else will enter.
In a mirror,
sleep is remembered as death

while combing the hair slowly
or unbuttoning a dress
heavy with shells,
or painting the fingernails
sea-blue.

And the dead? They won't be singing
or sunning themselves on rocks
when I pass, asleep
in the square hull of a boat
without sails.

2

In the mirror, a body like this one
only streamlined,
featureless as the sea,
the one who sleeps on a bed of shells,
the one with snails in the hair,

the one who lives in a house
of water,
the one I dream of, nudge aside

or stun,
the one I stone in my sleep with shells,

the one who sings to water—
it's as if the water were turning away
a glass ear,
disappointed to find itself
a sea.

3 · *Pericles*

And he walked home
carrying a basket of shells.
And when he rearranged them,
they were a face,
the face of a beautiful woman.

He fell in love.
He had no regrets,
though for days he returned to the shore
looking for the rest of the woman.
He found nothing.

The face, the model of my face,
a mask I wear at sea,
my mask of shells.
Now I have nothing covering me
when I see the drowned.

*

31

A man can keep walking
toward evening,
but he'll never get there,
not really, not the way
he'd like to.

An evening doesn't make
a country. The sky,
a few birds thrown in,
doesn't make a summer.
So a man keeps walking

toward evening,
but he only gets to the sea,
where he feels a certain disquiet.
As if the hand of someone drowning
had just touched his throat.

4

Mine is the voice in a sea-wall
overheard by a lighthouse again and again.
The fish don't notice
my beautiful wardrobe of stone . . .
Once, a girl was built

into a wall in Copenhagen.
She was chosen because her body was strong.
They piled stone after stone around her

as she wrote on a tablet and played
with her dolls,

until finally, the last stone
was placed overhead.
Though no one could hear her
playing inside, they knew she was there,
and with her eyes closed.

5

This is why the sky
has no regrets,
why people can lie
and we believe them,
the way the sea can lie

more openly to the land,
or how the drowned
have changed their names
so no one will know
who they are,

because the drowned
are famous and hiding
and don't want to be rescued.
I know this: they sink lower
when I pass.

6

You might say I'm unfamiliar
as the figurehead on the prow of a ship
as it passes over the stunned heads
of the drowned.
Or you might say the drowned are distant.

It's as if they were looking up
through a window they refuse to open.
So they could call out if they wanted to.
Or you might say they look peaceful
as they admire this woman.

They think of her as a wooden angel
passing over their heads, no light
from the blind eye. And she passes,
her expression unmoved
as the grain in wood.

7 · *Epilogue: A Fisherman's Story*

And if a whale were to swallow
the town,
would you stay in a belltower?
If you were a sexton,
would you go on ringing the bells?

Would the people keep talking,
drive cattle through the streets?
Would they eat fish?

Would the butcher make money?
Would the tailor sell suits?

And when the people
slit open the belly,
would the cattle and merchants
come spilling out, an odd parade
accompanied by bells, into the sea?

III

Upon Hearing of a Drowning in the Connecticut River

In silence, hope
Will live again even though hidden
With the seed under the snow.

Margherita Guidacci

Upon Hearing of a Drowning in the Connecticut River

That you once lived here
means nothing to the edge of the lawn,
nor to the shrubs
grown wild beyond your dying.
The marsh goes on
surrounding the fishing boats,
and the boats keep drifting away
past your terrible smile.
Leaves are lost,
or they are scattered like the shadows
around your address.
Your language has come and gone
like a knock at the door.
So the time has come
for the floorboards to be still
and for the windows to let your breath
go out into the rain,
because you are walking
somewhere else now.
And between here and wherever you are,
there is only this river
freezing over,
the water gradually hardening
into obsidian,
the stone bridge
sprouting shadows like weeds.
In the neighboring field,
two brown and white spotted horses
lean toward each other,
the thin smoke of their breath

rising in the cold . . .
There is only this winter.
You fell into it suddenly.
And now you are like the swallow,
those delicate bleached bones
beneath the elm tree.
Now you are like the fox,
that tattered fur
and black blood on snow.

The Marsh

Each time I return to this place
I expect to find a recurring distance
between myself and the huge trees,
as though I were in a dream
in which I could run toward them forever
and never get there.

Right now the marsh seems unfamiliar
because the crickets have taken me by surprise;
their singing has entered my mind just now,
even though I've been hearing them all along.
So I'm almost afraid,
because there must be other ways
in which I am left out of the landscape—
It's as if the mallards stay hidden in the grass
for a purpose. But I don't think they are there
to make me understand what I don't already know,
only to point out how often I'm surprised.
And that is why the mallards fly suddenly upward,
leaving the grass empty and essential.

And when I try to summarize the difference
between the tide and the way I remember it,
I find myself unable to explain
all that I have discarded—
The driftwood, fish skeletons
and chipped shells
are remnants of a past life
I can't possibly understand.

Winter Gulls

At first I narrow my eyes
because I think that maybe the gulls want more from me
than simply my observation of them,
but then I realize I'm mistaken,
it's just that they are usually thought of as beautiful,
while to me they look like scraps of dirty cloth
as they flap about over a dead fish left on the dock.
On another day, I might have exorcized them
more easily from my mind, or I might have walked
out to the wet rocks and thought again of all the years
the rocks and the tide have stayed
unmoved by each other. But today, it's as if the grass
doesn't want to be disturbed by anyone
walking too quickly, so I stay in one place
and keep staring at the gulls reeling over the fish.

And I think of myself as elsewhere,
how around me there are always other people,
and to them I am always *there* but never *here*,
and it seems to me that this is a terrible tragedy
like losing a best friend,
though everyone keeps talking nevertheless
or calling to each other over what they think
is the not too serious distance between them.
But sometimes, like now,
I can feel that distance becoming acute—
It's as if I were asleep
and trying to open my mouth.

Owning a Dead Man

The geese fly off, but sometimes they don't take
their voices with them. Stretched out like this,
I think my future is simple, like a cornfield
filling with light. I'm happy,
because of the way the geese have left their shadows
drying on the lawn around me, and the way
the long docks lean out into the water,
letting the unpainted boats knock against them.
Once, my mother told me, a woman came to this place
with an urn that held her dead husband's ashes.
The woman's pale hands tossed bits of gray-white
bone and soot onto the marsh, where the quail hid.
My mother was angry that the bones had trespassed
her land. *In a way*, she said, *I own a dead man.*

Now as I lie here, I think of the coming winter,
of his bones, mixed with the bones of the mouse
and the gull, cleansed and shining in the new snow,
but if I try to think too deeply, it's as if a bird
were pulling straws from a dried out nest!
So I wonder if I have ever witnessed the middle
of winter: the birch trees' inability to lose
anything more, or if I have ever seen myself
as more irrelevant than in December—
In that cold and stillness, my blood
and my muscles contracting as I tramp through the snow
couldn't possibly mean anything. And there *are* days
when a landscape feels nothing for its real trees,
only for what lies still in the snow,
or only for what has been.

A Burial, Green

It was afternoon, and my brother split
a turtle's head
open in the rain; the tiny skull
glistened, and soon the ants knew
every detail of cracked shell.
For hours he sat in the blue shade
of the elm, planning a burial
for his small dead, until
the shadows knew each curve
of grass around the green and orange
spotted shell, a tiny helmet
filling with air. It was spring
and the bark on the dogwood trees
was slick and wet, the cardinals twittered
on the green feeder.
And my brother thought it was ceremony,
the way the door to our white house opened
and he entered, done with his spade
and boots, the way my mother
hovered in the doorway
and touched his shoulder
without a word
like the rain.

Landscape

The grass is not yet drained of color
and the birds are flying low, as before rain.
The landscape has the look of something
looked at too long, a vanity by which things
know themselves. As a mirror knows.
In August, you have found the day
full grown as a crop you are afraid to harvest.
You are the raven afraid of the ash tree,
or the snake which tries to coil itself
around a stream of water. Though it tries
and tries, the air is still as futile,
just as gray. Can you think of another
landscape like this one, of a pond
as black and obscure? The faces
in the water float easily as leaves, or now
they are blown about like bits of burnt paper.
This is the only landscape you know—
the wind, obligated to fill the curtain
by your window, and the ashes on the sill
knowing vaguely what they were.

Dusk

I cannot worry
about what lies beneath the surface,
so I walk into the fragile dusk,
breaking the backs of field mice
still asleep under the snow.
The sunlight that does not reach me
illuminates the distance
between this world and God's,
where winter is simply the white
of perfect concentration.
I would like to believe in God,
just as I would like to believe there is an angel
weeping beneath the Chinese elms,
but He is an abstraction, like forgetfulness
or mathematics. In the mind of God,
winter can be summarized as one dark tree!
And yet, as I walk out over the frozen pond,
the pure white of this winter
enters my mind, and I become more open,
like a clearing in the woods
where light accentuates the dead underbrush
without emphasizing its ugliness.
And so I can live with my faults.
I can be touched
and not feel like a passing shadow.

The Land As It Is

1

You know that moment; the skaters decide
to abandon the ice when the rain has come
to cover over the old circles.

2

Things should stay in their places for a long time:
the bear inside the body it can't escape,
the eyes sewn shut and covered with buttons.

3

I think the name should be an object stored
in the locked room of a museum,
the eyes of the Egyptian statues going blank

4

when they hear it, a word so round and hard
it could be polished and placed in the mouths
of the dead to keep them from talking.

5

If he could, the bear would be moving away
through a maze of air and trees; he would know
with his eyes closed, the right direction.

6

The lake would still be the same,
have the same mournful look, the misfortune
of ice growing thin at the edges.

7

I could go further out into the rain,
past the flattened shadows of rocks and ferns,
past the speckled body of rain into nothing,

8

until the land appears as it is:
simply the roads with the fields between.

Beneath the Beech Trees
for my mother

In winter you began to forget yourself
and little by little you grew confident
until you were no longer afraid of the future
which like a wheatfield in snow
seemed a place of exile.
And every morning seemed new to you
like the first day of marriage
and you spent those days quietly,
wrapped in the invisible chrysalis of yourself.
But then one day you began singing
and the voice was sad as a prisoner's.

As we walked through the winter garden,
you pointed out that according to summer
we are extinct, and that each season
is unable to acknowledge any other
because they exist back to back.
But soon you became quiet
upon hearing the cries of the grackles,
as though you thought they had flown here
from another world.
Or maybe you thought they had traveled
the distance between you and the landscape.

It didn't matter whether the grackles
were meaningless or full of meaning,
they weren't even a point of reference!
Nor does it matter now
how lost you look beneath the beech trees,
though to you the trees may seem prophetic

49

because they live much longer than you do
and have a more direct connection
to the future.
Yet here they are, and here you are.
And you're holding your own.

Poem in Which I Am an Old Woman

> I am a word
> in a foreign language—
>
> Margaret Atwood

I am a word in a foreign language,
but I don't know what the word is,
so I sit here quietly,
an alien to my name.
Around me, the hedges rustle.
Finches settle on the roof,
unaware that nothing has changed,
that the field has been plowed again,
holding the seeds inside it like a secret.
And if there were a secret to be told,
it would be my name in another language,
uttered like a prayer for rain,
the rain that is falling beyond me
in another country, the clouds drifting
toward another year.
Now the finches scatter all at once.
There *is* a connection
between myself and their cries:

If bird cries or shadows
or too many barns on a hillside are confusion,
then maybe I should continue to live
in confusion.
But now it's as if the dusk
doesn't have meaning anymore,
which makes me want to turn inward
like a rose turning to ashes,
or become next to nothing
like the thin reeds.
Instead, I'm more like the brown snake,

its color so obvious that it seems to rub off,
a fine powder, onto the white stones
until nothing of me is hidden,
no part of me is crouched in the long grass.
And yet I can't see everything.
I can't know how exalted the owl feels
as it becomes what it is
by navigating the air,
by closing in on the mouse,
though like the mouse I have learned
I am not acceptable to everything.
I'm not acceptable to the grass
which, in this wind, seems to lean away from me,
and somehow closer to the end of my life.

IV

The Night Won't Save Anyone

Darkness arrives
splitting the mind open.

Something again
is beginning to be born.

Muriel Rukeyser

Soon This Poem Will Become Transparent

I would love to give myself back to the night
so that my naked body could become inarticulate
but loud like the sun.
I'm tired of thinking about myself,
which is too much like looking through a window
at a distant figure surrounded by purple shadows
and dead elms.
I'm tired of letting my fear change shape
like furniture in the dark.
I should ignore it,
because fear is arbitrary and could just as easily
stalk a hare in the moonlight
or become a shiver in the spine of a dog;
it could just as easily be like the wind
that slips my mind and enters a rosebush.

*

I feel as though the wind has returned
to the room I slept in as a child
and is breaking certain meaningful objects,
hurling a portrait from the wall,
tossing my favorite glass animals from the shelf,
as though my past is being disturbed
by what has never happened to me.
But I should not be afraid.
My past will change again.
Certain events will become important,
while others will recede
the way small dark houses in summer

seem to recede after a rain,
only to be replaced by the shiny street
and the smell of wet tar.

*

Soon this poem will become transparent
and I will be visible again.
My gestures will no longer be variations on a theme,
but the raising and lowering of hands.
I will be thinking outloud,
and the night will hear me as it climbs the hill
and slips into the orchard.
Sometimes the white almond trees seem to flare up
beneath the stars,
but tonight the clouds have come
as if from a great distance.
Soon the night will begin its prayer of rain.
I can speak to the night.
But it won't tell me how to live.

The Vanishing Street

It is still possible to imagine the landscape uncomplicated
by our idea of beauty,
just as it is possible to imagine that before the alphabet,
our emotions were simply stones that darkened
in each other's hands.
Of that time, I know very little,
only that once there was a night in which our failures
became stars we could choose to acknowledge
or abandon.
And if that night will never come again,
I must try to live in the present,
although there is no real present,
only the hidden arrangement of events
that, as they occur, determine
whether or not certain cloud masses will develop,
which trees will fall or not fall
outside the circle of our attention,
and whether a particular wind will signify
a more general spiraling out of emptiness
or merely disturb the curtains
by my window.
So my present contains its outcome,
just as sometimes I can know, before having spoken,
all possible routes of the conversation.
Yet it is also an assertion of how my past
does not belong to me,
but to those I have lost,
who each have absorbed a part of my past
into their own conceptions,
so that I am alone here

with the left-over fragments, difficult to reassemble,
in the way that it is difficult to reconstruct from memory
the exact positions of the houses,
lampposts and elm trees on the street where I live,
once the night has fallen, and I am drifting
into sleep, past the border of my room,
into the cool backyards.

The Burning Calendar

I feel as though I have lost the key to the house
where I am still a child
sleepwalking toward a long flight of stairs,
and I must watch helplessly as that remote self
falls into oblivion.
There is no end to such falling.
Nor is there an end to my turning inward,
which has left the autumn day to itself.
By deserting the last yellow leaves that persist,
I have caused them to become what they are—
objections made by a disinterested season.
So I am responsible
for the way the afternoon seems to have made a wrong decision
as it enters my thoughts,
which immediately dismiss it as *light*,
as tangential to the subject.
I am responsible for the way the grass seems to be a witness
when I search its name for something more
than green silence,
and for the way the woods as they lose color
are an expression of the distance between seasons.
So I cannot blame this day
for presenting itself as a kind of history of individual afterthoughts
that take a little time to be accepted as facts!
Nor can I blame it for not assenting to be easily summarized as
a square on a calendar,
especially since the hours cannot be reduced—
they are not empty and inexhaustible like the terms of an equation.
And yet, as I analyze myself,
I find that I can be simplified:

I am an equation in which the integers are
destroyed things,
that achieve balance.
And though not all that I have wished for will come true,
since I won't outlive my body,
which never will become a symbol for pure touch,
in my poems I can step out of myself
long enough to say that my blood is *a symbol* for pain.
And I can recognize that the change in season
can be caused by an instant in which nothing fails,
even though I am part of the change.

No Such Thing

In another world, there may be utterances
that remind you of slow carriages
vanishing into the distance of the approaching night,
but in this one, no such thing happens.
The sky is always what it is.
Yet it is also what broods above you as though sorry
for the interference of clouds and rain.
You have always taken the weather for granted
and have never questioned the blatant, aggressive wind . . .
There is a curious emptiness about the moon tonight,
as if it were planning to cast
no more round reflections.
Of course, it is difficult to decode its private language,
just as it is difficult to be sure that beyond one wheatfield
lies another, so that your thoughts can never flow easily
as from wheatfield to wheatfield to wheatfield.
So you must accept yourself as contradictory
because even though your thoughts are erratic,
you are always constant,
but in the way that one wave follows another
to a distant shore. In other words,
what you are is never quite as permanent as silence
or the granite sky. What you are is never quite as still
as the woods after a rain.
Therefore you must accept a part of yourself
in which your name is a foreign word,
in which the syllables you utter are the ticks of a clock
heard by no one,
because it doesn't matter that spiritual progress
isn't always like dressing in the half-light

61

in anticipation of going forward into a new day,
and because you *are* destined to be concealed in a body
that doesn't stroll casually down the street, laughing with others,
admiring the sunset.
So, you should surrender to yourself
as to a protective shadow.
You should forget that your life will eventually change direction,
like the needle of a compass toward true north.
You should proceed with caution, as though you were an endless
    night
scarcely touching the earth.

The Night Won't Save Anyone

Someday our bodies will no longer matter,
and we will leave them in our sleep, to travel easily.
But until then,
I will tramp like this through the woods
and not worry that this is the same snow
that falls gently between us—
What separates people
happens by accident, like unexpected weather,
and it is also caused
by the fact that there is always another handshake
to be done without,
always another unnecessary embrace.
It's the way there are those extra pear trees over there
next to those extra houses, which one day
will be abandoned.
In one of them, a man and a woman are kissing.
Sun is pouring in through the windows,
and behind them a gold paper fan is spread out
on the mantlepiece.
Now I realize they are my parents,
and everything seems suddenly empty.
Or maybe I'm afraid of losing what never happens
by having it happen.
I turn away.
It has grown darker.
The crows are where they aren't supposed to be,
on the scarecrow.
The horses have already forgotten what daylight is.
The swallows are leaving.
A dried nest falls from the barn.

The smell of damp hay.
Steam rising from manure.
The boy ringing a bell doesn't care if I listen.
He doesn't mind if I come up to the house,
or sleep each night on a torn sack in the barn.
I admire his indifference.
But how quickly the sun sets on this page!
The night has a certain, how shall I say it, *style:*
it is not concise and reminds me of
my own poems.
And the night won't save anyone.
It has another life, as I do, outside the poem,
and in that life, there isn't any landscape,
just the mind doing its work,
the mind which always wants to cling to such things as
deer trotting through rain,
while at the same time wanting to be rid of them.
It's the way I try to visualize my childhood friends
and they grow smaller, as if I am walking away from them.
Their faces begin to dissolve in a spiral.
I should have left them alone.
This has happened before.
Sometimes, while I am sitting in my room reading,
my mind will pass through the book
the way water passes through a grid and eventually finds itself
joining a river
which silently passes from town to town
by the factories and stockyards.
I turn the page.

The shade deepens on the lawn.
I can remember the way I felt as a child
when I would go out into the woods and think of myself
as invisible.
I was convinced I could become part of the foliage.
Now I often feel the reverse,
as though I stand out in a landscape,
a scarecrow in a burned field.
This makes me wonder if most people
think that winter is like an equation
to which they are being added.
Or maybe, to them, the sky is just so much whiteness.
If so, they are better off,
because they don't have to spend their time
wanting to be the perfect silence after a long rain,
nor do they have to worry about feeling overlooked
by the birch trees.
Instead, they can look into themselves.
But when I look into myself,
I feel as though I am looking into a pond in which the water
is hiding something,
the bones from last year's drowning, the split jaw,
the cracked skull.
I must go on admiring myself,
though it's the same as admiring a sunset
which is to be feared because of its nakedness.
And I go on believing that these words are real,
that they want to signify more than the rainy sky
or the early October evening.

But as I say each one, it looks for something concrete
the way grief goes looking for a dead loved one,
or the way a wind scavenges through yellow leaves,
looking for the visible part of itself.

Other Titles in the Contemporary Poetry Series